To

MW01265279

Sheila

HeartBroken

Now Healed and Delivered

From: Evangelist

Author

Teresa Tarply

Teresa Tarpley

With Lisa Bell

GOD Bless

Copyright © 2016 Teresa Tarpley

Published by Radical Women, bylisabell.

ISBN: 0692583734
ISBN-13: 978-0692583739

DEDICATION

This book is dedicated to hurt and broken people. God is able and faithful.
"So the last shall be first, and the first last: for many be called, but few chosen." Matthew 20:16 KJV

CONTENTS

ACKNOWLEDGMENTS

First giving thanks and honor to the Father, Son and the Holy Ghost for keeping your shield and protection around me, saving and delivering from life's tragedy and trauma.

And to all the people who hurt and harmed me. I want to say thanks. If I wouldn't have gone through the healing process, I wouldn't be able to say I forgive you or help others who need healing.

"And when ye stand praying, forgive, if ye have ought against any: that your Father also which is in heaven may forgive you your trespasses. But if ye do not forgive, neither will your Father which is in heaven forgive your trespasses." Mark 11:25-26 KJV

I am convinced that, except in a few extraordinary cases, one form or another of an unhappy childhood is essential to the formation of exceptional gifts.

Thornton Wilder

CHAPTER 1

FIRST MEMORIES

I came to life after my ninth birthday. On some days during my life, I wondered if nonexistence was better.

Perhaps I should see the missing pieces of my life's puzzle as a blessing, but I can't say for sure. I simply have little recollection of that time.

Of course, I didn't enter the world as a 9-year-old. I have pictures of myself as a small girl to prove I lived before then, so I know it's true. But the memories of my life before turning nine survive only in the deepest recesses of my mind, hidden from conscious thoughts.

The few images in my brain that make their way to the surface trouble me. I let those internal pictures surface on rare occasions, although I don't understand and often don't want to look at them. Nevertheless, the glimpses peek out at times, barely enough substance for me to feel certain about their truth.

A little girl huddled in her coat—head hanging so far down the collar concealed all but the top of her head. Slumped shoulders, she moved slowly through life, walking carefully so as not to disturb anyone. Always, this little girl wanted to please everyone around her.

Tough assignment for one so small.

She behaved as well as possible, filled with fear of what other people might say about her. A slight smile tried to peer out from whatever covered her face, but it never remained for long.

I see the picture clearly in my memory, but wonder. Who was this little girl? A sense of familiarity tugs at me. This little child, begging someone to notice her, yet scared. If they saw her, and she didn't please them…

Prickles run along my arms. I dare not finish the thought. I was that little girl, but I scarcely know her.

Morsels of information intrude, a moment of the past breaking into the present. When I think of that strange little girl—that former me—I remember little joy and a great deal of sadness. I don't remember why.

But ahhhhh—summer. Summer sun bathed me with warmth, and for a few months, I knew a bit of happiness. Then leaves fell, the sun disappeared behind gray clouds as cold wind blew in from the north. The tiny slivers of happiness flew away, caught on the breezes. As cold wind swept across the yard, depression returned. The leaves spiraled to the ground, meaningless and worth nothing. Not even a trip to the curb in a trash bag. Left alone where they landed, they simply died. I crunched them underfoot, tracking them into the house, a nasty unintended action.

My head and shoulders drooped again under the weight of working so hard to keep everyone in my life pleased—and frequently missing the mark.

So young, I didn't understand. No person could be perfect all the time. I didn't know I couldn't please some people, no matter how perfect I acted. And I had not yet learned the heaviness a child bears alone when she keeps trying to fill the role of pleasing everyone all the time.

Before my ninth birthday, I learned to be a people pleaser, but I didn't know how to be a happy child.

I experienced my first hurts, and pieces of my heart broke when I didn't fulfill an unrealistic expectation for myself. I failed at pleasing everyone, and no one told me I didn't have to.

Yes, God blessed me with missing pieces of my life. The puzzle without the entire picture hurt my soul enough. The unhappy child reminds me of one simple fact—I don't have to remember all of the early traumatic events for them to leave an imprint. All of the details seared in the lower layers of my brain still colored my choices.

When you can't remember life before 9 years old, and really don't want to, you know you're living heartbroken.

Bear and endure: This sorrow will one day prove to be for your good.

Ovid

CHAPTER 2
LIFE BEGINS

Fort Worth, Texas—where at one time cowboys herded cattle down Main Street to the stockyards. A place filled with museums, theaters and beautiful flower gardens. Where animals played in the zoo and water danced in a downtown area. The place where I entered the world.

We lived in the Butler Projects, where my only good memories of childhood happened. Even though I don't remember much about the early days of my life, an inkling of happiness lived there with us. Then I turned 9 years old, and that's where the memories start.

Mama met a man. Whether I liked him or not didn't matter. Mama did. When they got married, we left the only place I knew. We moved into a four bedroom, two-bathroom home with my stepfather and two brothers. Up until that time in my life, I didn't remember seeing such a wonderful house, much less live in anything close to that big or nice. But having a nice house didn't make it home.

Birthdays came and went, seldom accompanied by parties. Vague recollections of celebrations at my aunt's house tugged at the corners of my mind. But no one came to our house. We couldn't invite friends over, and the thought of a birthday party…

We didn't even ask the question. Outside of the house, we kept everything a secret. Mama always told me to keep my mouth closed and not tell nothing. I didn't know why and dared not ask. I didn't care if it was nice and big. I hated living in that house and wanted to go back to the projects. But Mama wasn't about to leave.

I never understood why, but somehow when we left the projects, all the family violence began. My brother, mother and stepdad fought every day. The new environment made me sad. I didn't

like the constant fighting. I did my best simply to
stay out of the way, which wasn't difficult most
of the time. Living in the backdrop caused me
pain, but sometimes I welcomed invisibility. The
orders to keep my mouth shut swelled, especially
when it came to talking about the abuse.

Mama constantly built up my brother and his
successes. Everything was about JR—always. JR
loved sports, and he did well. I stood by listening
as she talked to neighbors or family members.

"Did ya see what JR did in the game? He's
gonna go far."

I waited for just a mention. "Look, Mama, I
got an A on my report card."

She kept talking about my brother. "He's a
smart kid. Gonna do well in life."

My heart cried out to her, a pit of agony
begging for one word of praise. As much as I
tried to keep her happy, I never did enough to
please her. I wilted into the background while she
celebrated every single success for him. No
matter how well I did in school, she didn't
acknowledge me. So I tried harder, always
wanting to please her.

Why did she push me into the background,
always shining the light on my brother and never
onto me? Just once, please notice me. I couldn't
voice the words embedded in a hollow place of
my brain. What was so wrong with me? Didn't

she love me just a little bit? An invisible wedge grew between JR and me. The more she praised him and put me down to others, the bigger that wedge grew. I didn't care whether we ever became friends.

But my brother, Glen—oh how I loved him. We talked about everything, best friends. He didn't care if I was half his age. Even when he approached adulthood, ready to leave home, he still loved me. I never doubted him. The one constant in my life kept me steady, in spite of my mother's behavior toward me.

Then one day, the phone rang. I didn't mean to eavesdrop, and afterward I wished I didn't hear a second of the conversation.

"Yes, I have a son named Glen." Mama paused. "No. That can't be true. He was just here. What happened?"

The room swirled around me. What happened? Where was my Glen? Minutes passed, maybe only seconds. A silent roar rushed through me, muffling the conversation. Mama looked pale, grasping for something to hold and finding nothing.

Her voice rose, insistent. "But he's okay, right? He's gonna be okay."

Another pause and she grabbed her belly. Screams broke through the fuzziness washing over me.

"No," she screamed. "Nooooooo."

Wails pierced that big house as Mama slid down the wall. Thickness covered my vision while I watched her drop until her knees hit the floor.

I pressed my hands against my ears pushing away the moans coming from my mother. Pushing back what I knew wasn't good news. Pushing back thoughts that I didn't want to believe, but somehow knew were true.

Glen? Gone? I silently begged to be wrong, for him to be okay.

I tiptoed to my mom. "What happened?"

For once, she noticed me. Or maybe she said what she desperately wanted to deny, but had to believe. "Glen was stabbed in the back. It ain't good."

Mama didn't move. She stayed on the floor, the wails giving way to deep sobs. My brain tried to take hold of something that made sense. But nothing in my young world seemed right any longer. My chest hurt, heaving, begging for breath. Don't cry, don't cry. Crying means he really is gone. He can't be gone. I won't believe it. I won't. I forced the tears back, refusing to admit the truth. We'd get to the hospital and Glen…

A clothesline hung across the room. I pushed against it with all of my strength, not knowing what else to do. No one comforted me, and the one who always did wasn't there.

We headed to the hospital, a short ride that seemed to take hours. We had to get there. I had to see him, will him to live. But by the time we got there, Glen was gone.

The doctor's words rang through my ears, embedding in some secret place of my brain. I wished I didn't hear him—that somehow not hearing erased the truth. But I heard. And the words confirmed the torturous reality.

"I'm sorry. We did everything we could. They stabbed him in the back and it hit his heart. He was DOA. We couldn't do anything."

I pressed fingers into my ears. No. Not my best friend. He couldn't be gone. He couldn't be. But he was. And nothing would ever be the same again.

In three words, I can sum up everything I've learned about life.

It goes on.

Robert Frost

CHAPTER 3

LIFE GOES ON

Glen's death changed me forever.

From that day forward, the very thought of death terrified me. How could this happen? How could Glen die? If he wasn't safe, then maybe I wasn't either. All the time we lived in the projects, I never knew that kind of fear. Other people thought of the projects as dangerous. People died there. But we didn't live in the projects anymore.

All I remembered from the projects was good. I had fun there with friends and neighbors who were more like family. We played on the merry-go-round, walked a bridge to visit the gym. And we watched out for each other. The projects meant safety to me—much more so than the fancy house where we now lived. I wanted to go home.

Nightmares plagued me. Even the thought of a funeral sent my mind reeling. When we watched the movie Roots, I sobbed while the slave owner beat Kunta Kinte. Just a movie, yet so real. Every blow stung my back.

How could things possibly get worse?

Soon after my brother's murder, Mama joined a small Baptist church. She dragged me along, but I didn't like it much. Every time we went, I felt like they were trying to force me to do what they wanted. It reminded me of my stepdad always telling me exactly what to do and not do.

They always tried to talk me into joining something. They wanted me to take part in this group or that. Some of the kids there weren't nice to me, and bad things happened whenever we went. At least it seemed bad to me. Church was supposed to make me feel good, but I felt terrible by the time we left. I wanted nothing to do with anyone there or any of their many activities.

The people in that church didn't talk much about Satan. At that time, I still pictured him as a little red man with horns. He didn't particularly seem tough and certainly didn't appear dangerous. He felt more like a nuisance. Yet, maybe he stood there instigating some of the bad I experienced. Maybe he wanted me to stay away from church because he had a sense that God wanted something special for me.

Whatever the reason, he won. I quit going to church with Mama, and she let me.

Before long, my stepdad put out my other brother, JR, demanding he didn't even come on the street. Confusion invaded what little sanity I had left. Who was this unstable man my mother chose to marry? Mama and I already lost Glen, so why did my stepdad do this to us? JR was barely 18. Even though Mama built him up all the time, ignoring me, I loved him at some level. We didn't have the close relationship I knew with Glen. But he was still my brother.

After that, the violence really started, and my stepdad controlled everything. He gave us a separate phone line and we never used his phones. He put in a separate refrigerator. We didn't eat from his food supply, and we sure didn't eat at the same time as he did.

Every night, we followed a strict routine, eating at precisely the same time, not a minute before or after. He expected us to eat at our assigned time, or we didn't get supper. No plate saved if we happened to come in later. We didn't eat as a family. He never ate what Mama cooked, and we didn't dare eat anything he prepared.

We took a bath before dark, or we didn't bathe. We dared not come home late. This was true for both Mama and me. He treated her like a child, controlling her as much as he did me.

Every night the same thing happened. My stepdad came home in a foul mood. The stench of beer followed him into the house, mingling with his Winston cigarettes. The smells gagged me, but I never complained about it. An alcoholic, any small infraction of the way he thought things should go resulted in severe punishment. He beat my mom physically and mentally abused her on a daily basis. I watched, thinking of Kunta Kinte, wanting to make him stop, but not big enough to do anything.

Even though I went to school every day, I didn't talk about what went on at home. Telling would make it worse.

My stepdad didn't allow her family to come over. If we wanted to see them, we had to go to their house. Before long, Mama started sharing my room.

She didn't talk about how to keep myself clean or why I should bathe, brush my teeth and hair.

She took little interest in whether I wore clean clothes or the same ones for days in a row. All I knew about boys came from others, not from my mother. What she taught me left a warped idea of marriage and love.

Oh if we could only live in the projects again. I thought back to those times when we had less money, but life felt right. I loved visiting my aunt, who still lived there. During those times, peace flowed over me. But it never lasted. The minute we went back to the big house, turmoil rose up all around me. Why couldn't we break free from the tyrant of a man?

One night, the abuse broke out as usual. I don't know what he got so mad about, but he unleashed brutality on Mama harsher than I ever saw before that night. Horror encompassed me. I wanted to make him stop. To end the madness. But as he delivered one blow after another, I retreated to a corner, terrified he might turn his fists on me. When the blows finally ended and he walked away, I helped my mom to her feet. We gathered a few things and slipped out the door, headed for my aunt's house.

Mama didn't say much. I didn't know what to say to comfort her, and no one comforted my wounded heart. Is that how a man is supposed to treat his wife? I didn't think so. Maybe the viciousness would force her back to the east side.

Oh please, God. Let this be the last time I see that house. I wanna be safe in our old place.

By the time we got to my aunt's house, exhaustion pulled me to bed and sleep. As I drifted off, my aunt's voice floated through the house telling my mom she needed to leave him. I agreed and hoped Mama listened.

Later that week, she applied for housing.

We're coming home. It's all gonna be okay now.

I couldn't contain my excitement. Mama took off one morning. She didn't say why, but I knew she needed a job. After about a week, she finally came back and picked me up. As we drove out of the east side, my stomach churned. Where were we going? We did have clothes and personal belongings at the house. That made sense. But we got there and stayed. What? Why aren't we leaving? Mama wouldn't talk about it.

A few days later, the phone rang, and I grabbed it.

"Hello, this is Ms. Smith. Is your mother at home?"

Ms. Smith? Ooooohhh. The lady from the projects. Maybe we have housing and we can leave. "Yes, she's here. Just a minute."

I laid down the phone and ran to find my mom. "Mama, Ms. Smith on the phone. She wants to talk to you."

"I don't want to talk to her," she said.

"You have to. She's waiting."

"Take a message. I'm too busy to come to the phone right now."

She sat there eating and watching TV. I hurried back to the phone, hoping Ms. Smith hadn't hung up on us. "She can't come to the phone. Can I give her a message?"

"Tell your mother her housing is ready. I really need to talk with her."

I covered the phone with my hand and yelled, jumping up and down inside. "Mama, come talk to her. We got a house. It's ready for us."

"I'm not talking to her."

"Please. You have to talk to her."

"No. Tell her not to call back and hang up."

Water filled my eyes, but I didn't let a drop escape. I didn't want to hang up. I wanted Ms. Smith to come save us. "My mother said to take your number," I lied. The churning in my stomach rose to my throat as I wrote down the number. If he beat her again, maybe she'd change her mind. He would—she probably wouldn't. But I held on to that tiny shred of hope.

I walked back to the living room. "Why did you do that?" I yelled. "Why did you turn down a new place for us to live?"

"It's none of your business," she replied coolly, focused on her snack and show.

I grabbed her arm. "It is my business. Why are you staying with him?"

"I'm not gone leave my house to go back to the projects."

"You can't possibly love him. Not after the way he's treated you."

"You think I married this man out of love? I wasn't in no love. I just wanted the money. I don't want to talk about it no more. You stand in the place of a child and shut yo mouth."

I stood still, stunned by a blow as real as if she slapped my face. She endured the beatings because of money? Something about that seemed so very wrong to my young mind. I vowed never to marry a man for his money—especially if it gave him the right to abuse my body and mind on a daily basis.

I stepped in front of the TV to get her attention. "When we left the projects, we moved from Heaven straight to Hell."

I ran to my room, slammed the door and collapsed on the bed before the tears pushed themselves from my eyes.

I'll never marry a man for his money. Never! I'll pay them instead. Then they will love me and never put their hands on me in a hurtful way.

At 10 years old, I made up my mind about what love meant. I'd rather live in the projects than stay with a man who constantly beat and controlled every move I made, every ounce of food I ate and when I went to bed or anything else for that matter. I'd never let a man control me like that.

Never!

From that day on, my mother embarrassed me. I didn't want anyone to see me with her. If they did, I lied about her identity. For some reason she got addicted to eating Argo starch. She didn't want to go in the store to buy it though, so she took me and insisted I go make the purchase. Riding in the back seat, I scrunched down if I saw anyone I knew.

Eating this stuff made her gain weight. She gained, and gained and gained some more. As if I wasn't embarrassed enough, I hated that she got so fat. I made fun of her with my friends and sometimes said, "She's pregnant." I sure wasn't about to tell anyone—absolutely no one—that she ate starch. How sick could she be?

Then again, she stayed with an abusive, controlling man. And that was the sickest part of all.

I never hate. I just sit back and wait on your turn.

Teresa Tarpley

CHAPTER 4
LIFE AT 14

My mother always told me if I had sex with a boy, I would get pregnant. She never told me if I had sex, I would get a disease. No one told me that tidbit of information.

Mama never celebrated my success. For some reason, she rewarded me for doing wrong no matter what. Whenever I did something wrong, she rewarded me. When I behaved the right way, she looked at me as if I did something wrong. I brought home a straight F report card, expecting to be in big trouble. Instead, she said, "Let's go shopping." They put me in special education classes. I often fell asleep in class, confused and not understanding anything. My teachers didn't explain things well. If it hadn't been for Glen, I would never have learned to read.

Before Glen's death, he helped me all of the time. Without him, math left me in a fog. I was in summer school and not doing well, but I didn't admit that to my family. Instead, I convinced them my math grades had improved. Mama yelled at me. Why? Shopping for F's, but anger when I told her I improved in math? How did that make any sense at all?

One day, JR answered the phone and found out the truth from my teacher. We didn't get along very well. Mama always pushed him to the forefront. He always stood out, no matter where he went, and she shone with pride when she talked about his successes—in sports, grades, popularity. He was always out and about while Mama wouldn't let me off the front porch. I never measured up to him, never good enough to get a taste of the praise Mama gushed with over him.

But that day, JR sat down with me and taught me how to add and subtract. "You have to be able to do basic math at least," he said.

I cringed against what surely was coming. But he didn't make fun of me. He didn't call me names. On that one occasion, he took time to teach me. I learned basic math that day—but only that one time. I appreciated the help, but it didn't end my feelings of intimidation nor did the one-time event deepen our relationship.

In the meantime, Mama kept repeating the thing about having sex, accusing me of getting with the guys. Who could think about sex with so much confusion over schoolwork? I reverted to making bad grades to keep her from ragging on me. At that point I was still a virgin, but if she wanted to accuse me of sleeping around, why shouldn't I?

I met this guy—so hot and popular. I melted if he ever looked my way. My tongue tangled in my mouth. I didn't say much around him, terrified any words would come out mispronounced and sounding like a moron. No way would I make a fool of myself.

All the girls wanted to get with him. What chance did I have? None of the boys paid attention to me, so he sure wouldn't. He could have any girl he wanted, and most of them would do whatever he wanted to do. But then, he started paying attention to me. Me. Of all the girls around, he wanted me. The bad grades, bullying and constant misery at home disappeared into the clouds under my feet.

One day, we sat around talking. "Do you wanna hook up?"

I thought for a minute. I knew what he meant by hooking up. I wasn't totally naïve. My mother's words played through my mind like a scratched record. Would I really get pregnant if I had sex? And who cared if I did anyway? Maybe Mama lied to me. Maybe she just didn't want me to enjoy life. I hated everything about her. Still…

"I'm not on any birth control. My mama won't get it for me." I wasn't quite sure if I was ready for this.

"We'll be careful. I don't want no kid." His laughter soothed the nervousness and at the same time made me wonder about doing it. "C'mon, baby. You're my girl. Don't you love me?"

I wasn't sure what love looked like, but I sure wanted to be his girlfriend. No one bullied me or made fun of me. I was with the hottest guy at school.

"Okay," I whispered, with the squeaking sound of a mouse caught in a trap.

We sneaked away that afternoon, and I lost my virginity to him.

A week later, he wanted to have sex again. I didn't hesitate the second time. He must love me if he wanted to get with me again. I never considered that my actions didn't make him respect me. He took me to a garage and didn't waste any time getting me stripped. In the middle of having sex, voices filtered through the door. Some of his friends called out his name. He just kept going, ignoring everything but his pleasure.

Suddenly the garage door flew up, and they walked in on us. He got up and left. The guys laughed and took my clothes.

"Give my clothes back," I screamed.

The boys laughed harder, playing keep away as I tried to cover myself and grab for anything to put on. Some ran out of the garage, twirling my clothes above their heads. I looked for my boyfriend, but he was nowhere in sight. I'm not sure which hurt more—the humiliation of being caught in the act, or that the one I thought loved me abandoned me.

For more than an hour, the boys played their little game, at one point leaving with my things. I sat down, sobbing, ashamed and embarrassed. Finally, they gave my clothes back, making fun of me and calling me a crybaby. I got dressed and ran.

Back at school, word traveled like an out-of-control freight train. My so-called boyfriend never officially broke up with me, but if I even saw him in the hallways, he ignored me. I tumbled into a deep depression. My reputation plunged with my mood. Several of the guys said we had sex, outright lying as I walked by. Sometimes another boy, or several of them, claimed they were all with me that day. None of it was true. Girls gave me dirty looks. Boys looked at me like hungry wolves wanting a taste of my flesh.

Weeks later, I got sick. I had to use the bathroom all the time, but when I did, it hurt and smelled gross. My throat was sore, and I had a fever. Joints all over my body ached. It sounded a lot like the flu, so I didn't worry too much. When I stood up one night, I screamed and grabbed my lower stomach.

"What's wrong?" Mama asked.

"It hurts really bad, Mama." I clutched my lower ab and fell down.

She came over and felt my forehead. "You're burning up. We're going to the ER."

"No. I don't want to go there." Thoughts of Glen twisted through my mind.

My mom pulled me up. "Don't be foolish. You have to see a doctor."

We headed to the ER even though I protested and lied about feeling better while I kept doubling over in agony.

After an extensive exam, blood tests, poking and prodding, the doctor came in the room. "Looks like gonorrhea, but we're running a culture to make sure."

Gonorrhea? What's that? I didn't have a clue.

Mama sat beside the bed, a dim light shining across her face. The depth of red crossing over it scared me. "So what do we have to do? Wait for the results?" The clipped tone of her voice rattled my nerves.

"We'll go ahead and get her started on antibiotics." The doctor started to walk out and then stopped and turned around. "These things happen. At least she isn't pregnant."

He left then, and I feared the words about to explode from my mother. I didn't know what gonorrhea was, but from the doctor's statement, I figured it must be something that came from having sex.

Mama didn't explode. Her voice came out tight and even. "Well I guess we'll have to make sure that don't happen. I told you not to be having sex."

Pregnancy was the least of my worries. The excruciating pain left me afraid to have sex again. I didn't ever want to do it again. The humiliation from the last time and then this... Why would I ever want to have sex again?

"I know, Mama. I'm sorry," I said. "More sorry than you know. I'll never have sex again." I spared her the details of my shameful experience.

She responded by staring me down, her eyes full of a sharp dagger-like glare. That look cut through my heart with a searing pain. I felt awful physically and inside. I messed up, but how could she be so cruel? Where was the shopping trip now? It came on the way home—at the pharmacy where she picked up two prescriptions. One for anti-biotics and another to prevent pregnancy.

Even though I feared sex like an epidemic of the worst kind, I took the birth control pills. Within a short time, I woke up sick to my stomach every morning, sometimes throwing up. I stayed tired.

"You didn't learn, did you?" Mama asked one day.

"What?"

"You're doing it again. You got with some boy and now you're pregnant."

"No, Mama. I'm not with anyone. I swear it."

"You're such a liar. Get dressed."

"Where are we going?"

"Just get yourself dressed. NOW."

Within an hour, we pulled up in front of an abortion clinic. What was she doing? I couldn't be pregnant.

"Mama, please. This is crazy."

"Shut up and get inside."

The nurses took a urine sample and directed us to wait in the lobby. I wiggled around, flipping thoughtlessly through a magazine. I got to the end, tossed it aside and picked up another.

Finally, the door opened. "Teresa Tarpley." The nurse smiled. I wanted to punch her.

In the exam room, the nurse turned to my mom. "The test is negative. Your daughter isn't pregnant."

A huge smile spread across Mama's face. "Thank you." She turned to me. "Let's go."

She didn't say anything else to me, but that smile never faded between the clinic and home. I wanted to swat the triumphant look from her face.

But I didn't. I stuffed the sorrow deep inside.

> Bullies want to abuse you. Instead of allowing that, you can use them as your personal motivators. Power up and let the bully eat your dust.

Nick Vujicic

CHAPTER 5

GETTING BULLIED FOR WHAT

There was a time my mother took me to church every Sunday. One particular usher always tried talking me into joining the usher board. I never quite understood why. I didn't trust him and even if I had, I didn't want to join anything at church.

I politely declined saying, "Maybe one day." But in the back of my mind, I screamed, "NOT!"

It seemed every time I went to church something bad happened. Someone lied on me and tried to get other people to fight me. One particular girl from the neighborhood, Shelia, set her sights on me. One of the younger girls, I didn't know her. She didn't know me either. We only saw each other in passing. But every time she saw me, she called over her friends and started a fight with me. Still to this day, I don't know why. I didn't want to fight, especially feeling clueless about the reasons behind it. So I got to the point when I saw her coming, I ran the other way. Then I stopped going to church. With all this hell going on, God couldn't be real. How could He stand by and watch this group of girls beat on me? What kind of God does that if he's real and powerful?

My dad's sisters talked about God all the time. Their language sounded foreign to me. Where was the glory and blessings they discussed? They didn't have a clue about my life or the terror that went on at our house. In time, I didn't want to hear about it anymore.

School wasn't any better. My reputation stunk. After my first sexual experiences and that horror, I kept my legs shut tight. But the lies and rumors continued.

After one mistake, I was marked as a slut. No one asked me if it was true. No one cared. Shame crept up my neck, climbed to my cheeks and planted a permanent heat of embarrassment. My head hung low—I noticed feet and dirty floors. But the words still pounded my brain, pushing my head deeper toward my chest. My shoulders slumped every day as I hustled out of school when the bell rang.

A black cloud hung over my mind. Nothing brought me joy. I dropped into a hole of depression, wondering if any part of life was good. I longed for the innocent days of the projects, knowing I could never have that life again where we played carefree all day. Even if we moved back now, my innocence was gone.

On the weekends, I headed to my aunt's house to get away from the bullying and church. My mother's sister didn't preach at me. We sat and watched soap operas. Misery hung over me, and I couldn't fight back the tears sitting at the surface of my eyes. They constantly leaked out.

One day as we sat there, I kept looking at the TV. The week was harsh, and the smallest thing threatened to open the dam behind my eyes. I didn't know how to explain why I cried, so if I hid them, Aunty wouldn't ask.

She didn't miss much.

"Teresa, what's wrong, Baby?"

"Nothing," I lied, shaking my head.

She pressed. "There's gotta be something. Why else you be crying?"

"It's nothing."

"Your stepdaddy messing with you, girl?"

I peeked over at her face then. Anger boiled in her eyes. Mama must have not told her about any of the other stuff. How could she? I never told her about what happened in that garage. I sure didn't tell her about what all the kids at school said about me.

I hesitated. I couldn't tell my aunt the truth. My neck heated up on the way to my face. I thought back to the day my stepdad locked me out of the house on purpose. He sat right there in the living room. I banged on the door and rang the bell for a long time. Finally, I plopped down on the step in the heat and cried.

Some friends asked me what was wrong.

"I wanna go inside, but the door is locked."

Someone said, "Ask your daddy."

A bellowing voice broke through the window pane. "I'm not yo daddy."

My aunt's gentle voice broke through the memory. "Well, is he?"

The lie came out so easily. "Yes."

Right then all my anger swelled up in the quiet answer. I didn't know what would happen in the wake of that one word. I didn't care. I hoped they carted him away, and maybe took my mama with him. Maybe then, I'd feel better. Nothing happened. Mama stayed with that man who wasn't my daddy, and life kept going the same way it always went.

Eventually Shelia went to juvenile—even then, it had nothing to do with me. The one piece of conflict went away, but my life didn't feel any better. Kids at school still bullied me, made fun of me and whispered behind my back or sometimes to my face.

I didn't want to come clean with my aunt and admit I lied about my stepdaddy. He did a lot of things, and I never liked him much, but he didn't touch me. I stopped hanging out on the East side and just stayed home on the weekends. Mama had her religion, and I guess somehow that made her feel better about the misery at home.

Still, no church for me. I wasn't going back. The church had nothing for me, and I sure didn't have anything to give them.

The thief does not come except to steal, and to kill, and to destroy. I have come that they may have life, and that they may have it more abundantly.

Apostle John (John 10:10 NKJV)

CHAPTER 6
IN LOVE AT 15

By my 15th birthday, the idea of having sex still scared me. But then I met this guy.

He recently moved into town. Finally someone who was going places. He wasn't a loser like my first boyfriend. This guy had things going for him. A job, training, education. I couldn't believe he wanted to be with me. I had my plan in place too. I would keep this one. He'd be my ticket away from Mama and my stepdaddy. I'd do what it took to keep him, but he wouldn't take care of me. I was gonna take care of him.

As soon as we started hanging out, he expected things from me. He didn't have to ask for sex. I knew he wanted it and before long, I gave in. My mama had me on birth control anyway, so I might as well do it. The memory of gonorrhea didn't frighten me anymore. After all, this guy was different. He loved me. He was really my boyfriend.

I asked someone one day, "You seen my boyfriend?"

He stepped out of the shadows. "What you talking about? I ain't yo boyfriend."

"No? You just messing around with me? Sound like a boyfriend to me."

Some of the people around us laughed, nodding heads in agreement. "She got you, man."

He answered back with a sneer toward our friends. Then he asked me, "You got any money? I need some cash."

I pulled a couple dollars from my pocket and gave it to him. Yeah, I had him. I was right. Give them money, and they'll stick around. We went off and had more sex. On Fridays after school, I always met up with my boyfriend. Whether he called himself that or not, we were a couple.

During the week, I skipped eating so I could save my lunch money. I wanted to get a job but

Mama said, "Girl, you don't need no job. I'm gonna take care of you."

She had no clue what I was doing.

When I met up with him, I handed over the money to last him until the next week. We went on this way for weeks that drifted into months. I didn't care. He was my love. The plan worked. I continued giving him my lunch money, we kept meeting up and going off to a back room. Being in love was so great. And my plan was far better than what I learned from Mama to let some man beat me just so he'd keep taking care of me. I controlled my boyfriend instead of him controlling me.

Months later, I started creeping around with his friends. I continued giving him my lunch money. His friends welcomed me. I didn't understand why they liked me so much, but before long, I found out. We'd been in the back, doing our thing. My boyfriend got up and went out. One of his buddies came in the room.

I pulled the sheet over me. "What's up?"

"Your man said I could have a turn with you. I ain't been with anyone in a long time."

I wasn't sure what to think.

"It's cool, baby. We're all gonna make you happy."

And they did. All of his friends roamed in and out that day. It became a regular routine. And my boyfriend didn't have any problems with sharing me. It didn't take too many days before I realized how out of control I was. He still took my money, but things changed.

He started beating on me. I can't remember why he beat me or what set him off the first time. I loved him though, so as his fist pounded on me, I took it. Just like Mama. My paying him didn't stop the pain.

Once he took me to a vacant building and beat me up bad. The string of names hurt as bad as the blows. I went to school with black eyes, making up some story so they didn't call the police. That should have been enough to keep me away, but I kept going back. If I didn't, he came looking for me.

His parents eventually moved him out of town. It broke his hold on me. The beatings stopped. I no longer creeped around with his friends. Although I was secretly glad to be away from him, I missed having a boyfriend. Who was gonna love me? And when did anyone get a chance?

My mom always said I had to be in the house before the street lights came on. She treated me like a baby, trying to do everything for me. Yet she didn't teach me how to take care of myself or about proper hygiene. By that time, I didn't want her to take care of me, but she insisted.

After a while, I got burnt out with that. She allowed me to go skating in the daytime on Saturdays. All my friends were going and hanging out at the skating rink at night. Why couldn't I hang out with them all the time? So after a while, I started making my own curfew. I came home when I got ready. I seldom made it to the house before dark, and if I did, it was only a stop off before going somewhere else.

I quickly got bored with the skating rink. I'd experienced more than most of the kids there. They skated around in circles, naïve to the real world.

I met some people that liked going to the clubs where all the smoking and drinking happened. That sounded more exciting than looping a building with wheels against a wooden floor. So I went with them. I wasn't old enough to get into the clubs, but I did. And the supply never seemed to run low. Yeah I was loving all that. My life didn't look so bleak against the loud music and partying atmosphere.

I started skipping school then. My body was theirs, but my mind wasn't.

Throughout life people will make you mad, disrespect you and treat you bad. Let God deal with the things they do, cause hate in your heart will consume you too.

Will Smith

CHAPTER 7
STILL SWEET 16

Being 16 wasn't so sweet. We had some neighbors who lived down the street from us. One of them was an old classmate in elementary. They used to call me player. I thought they were some cool people because they smoked cigarettes, smoked weed and drank beer. They didn't go to clubs. Ms. Sheryl was the head of the house. She asked me to have sex with her and her boyfriend. His name was Bubba. I really didn't want to, but for some reason, I couldn't tell people no.

So, I did it. My first of that type of experience freaked me out—I never wanted to do it again. Even though the whole experience left me uncomfortable, I continued to hang out with them. She never asked again, but every time I went there, I stuck close to the door so I could escape fast.

Ms. Sheryl tried to talk her niece into getting me to leave my house key with them so they could steal my mother's checks. I said no and never did leave the key with them. What a lesson to learn. You can't tell everything because of the thieves and dream killers.

A couple of weeks later, she had some guys at her house. Everyone was smoking weed and drinking beer. One of the guys liked me—I thought he did anyway. Somehow, the subject of cocaine came up. One of the women got up to leave. The talk of hard drugs left me jumpy, so I tried to leave behind her.

As I headed to the door, one of the guys slapped me. You ain't goin' nowhere. I spent my money on this dope and you think you gonna just up and leave without paying for it?"

"I don't have no money."

"I don't want yo' money."

He forced me to have sex and perform oral sex on him and his friend. Ms Sheryl opened the curtains and allowed her children and friends to watch. I left the house, humiliated. I'd never go back there again.

Never.

A few days later, Ms. Sheryl's niece found me and said Ms. Sheryl wanted to talk to me. I didn't respond. I hated the thought of going back to that house. Later that evening my mom and I sat in our room talking.

A knock on the door interrupted us. Ms. Sheryl's niece told me again that Ms. Sheryl wanted me. I couldn't tell Mama why I didn't want to go, so I went. Maybe they were sorry about what happened the last time I was at her house. I'd see what she wanted.

When I got there, one of the guys that took advantage of me waited. Not again. I turned around and bolted for the door, but he jumped in front of me, blocking the door so I couldn't get out.

"I just want to apologize," he said.

"That's it?" I crossed my arms, mostly to keep my hands from shaking. I swallowed hard.

"Yeah. That's all."

"Fine. I accept. Now move out of my way. Mama expects me back home."

I pushed past him, holding back tears until I got away from the house. He couldn't see my fear, couldn't have that power over me. I half-expected to hear his feet pounding the ground behind me. When I got home, my breath escaped after I closed and locked the door behind me. After all that you would think that would be enough. Not so.

People warned me about Ms. Sheryl. I never paid them any attention.

About a month later, I was hanging out with a lady named Tee. We had been smoking weed and drinking. She got out of the car.

"I got this money in my purse from pimping," I told her. I was only making slugs at an ex-pimp.

Less than five minutes later, Tee's friend came to the car. "Give me Tee's purse." I hesitated. He started cussing, hitting the car. I wasn't taking his violence. Tee wasn't worth getting beat up. I gave it to him.

The next day Tee walked toward me, accusation all over her face. "You stole my money."

"What? No I didn't."

"Really? You were in the car with my purse, and now all my money is gone. All of it."

I didn't have a clue she had money in her purse. "Oh my gosh. You're friend must've took it. He demanded your purse. I didn't want him to beat me up, so I gave it to him."

She glared at me. "Whatever."

I knew she didn't believe me, but I couldn't do

anything about it.

Later that evening Ms. Sheryl's niece called. "My friend said you were talking about us. Ms. Sheryl is pissed. You better get over here."

How would I get out of this one? I went over to explain myself. Somehow, I had to convince Ms. Sheryl I didn't mean anything bad by it. Tee was there as well. I wondered what she might have told them.

The next thing I knew, they dragged me into a room, beat me up real bad. Ms. Sheryl called people to come over. They gave her money to have sex with me. She kept me locked in the room until around 3:00 a.m. She opened the curtains for the whole neighborhood to watch. As they stood around, she beat me up again and made me perform oral sex on a handicapped man. If I tried to object, she hit me again. I wanted to run, but knew she had too many people to keep me from leaving.

Shame covered me. My body hurt from the blows. I don't know how many people went through the room. After a while, numbness swept over me as I begged Ms. Sheryl to stop and let me go. She kept bringing people through.

Tee came in and told me to perform oral sex on her as well, but she couldn't go through with it. More time passed. Tee and some of the other people talked Ms. Sheryl into letting me go.

Wow. I had two black eyes, busted lips, and scratches everywhere. Tee and some others took me to another woman's house. I didn't dare go home. Mama couldn't see me.

I slept for hours, then about 2:00 p.m., Tee and I walked to the store. Another of my friend's mother was there.

"Oh my Lord. Teresa, what happened to you?"

I tried to answer, but the shame bubbled up, choking out my voice. Tears formed and slipped down my cheeks.

"C'mon, Baby. I'm taking you home."

I got in her car, thankful I didn't need to worry about more pain or humiliation. She took me home to a locked, empty house. The lady prayed for me and helped me climb through the window in my stepdad's bedroom.

Mama eventually got home. When she came in my room, she started in on me. "Where were you all night? How dare…"

Suddenly her face flashed shock, quickly followed by controlled anger. "Who did this to you? What happened?"

I told her, leaving nothing out.

"I'm calling the police."

"No. They'll hurt me again."

"We'll take care of that."

She went to call the police. Secretly, I wanted

her to call them. I wanted her to make everything better. For once, she didn't ignore or blame me for what happened.

The police came, and I explained to the Tarrant County officer what happened. He wrote down Ms. Sheryl's address and asked for all the other names. I told everybody's name—at least the ones I knew. The officer said if I didn't I would be in trouble. Tee and some of the others begged me not to tell the cops on them. But I'd had my fill of trouble.

My mom packed our things and hid me out long enough for everything to blow over. I never heard what happened with that situation. Ms. Sheryl continued to live in her house, which I avoided as if she had multiple strains of flu going on there. She called my mom's house phone a year later asking about the company I kept. Mom wasn't telling her anything.

I finally realized, much later, these people were not my friends.

Being a teenager is hard.

Mae Whitman

CHAPTER 8

AGE 16 AND FEELING IT

One morning, I woke to the bright overhead light, my mom standing over me. I blinked against the light.

"What are you doing? It's still dark outside. Why you waking me up so early?

"I got a call from the school last night," Mama said.

"So. What are they lying about now?" I knew fully well why they called. I didn't remember the last time I cast a shadow across any of their doors.

"You haven't been at school in a long time, Teresa. You better not have been hanging out with those good for nothin' hoodlums, sleeping around, getting pregnant or sick again."

"I don't know what you're talking 'bout. I been at school."

"You sayin' they're lying to me? I believe them before I believe you. Now get your sorry self up outta that bed and get ready for school."

"I got plenty of time. I'm too tired to get up yet."

"If you didn't stay out all night you wouldn't be so tired."

With that, Mama came over to the bed and yanked the covers back. "I said get up," she shouted.

At that moment, anger bubbled up and boiled over. My heart picked up a faster rhythm, beating like a bass drum inside my head. "I don't need no school. They ain't teachin' me nothin' anyway. Why should I go?" I pulled the covers over my head.

"I'm not going to jail and paying a fine because you're being stupid."

Mama yanked the covers back again, and grabbed my hair, pulling me out of the bed and onto the floor.

"I hate you. You're such an embarrassment with yo fat self." The words slipped out and my jaw clenched tight. I grabbed her hand, digging nails into her flesh.

The fight was on. With her free hand, she slapped my face—hard. Sweat popped out all over my body as I swung wildly trying to break her hold on my hair. She pulled harder until I thought my scalp might explode. I latched on to her hand again and dug as deep as I could, while she pulled upward. My butt came off the floor and she punched me.

It seemed all the times she suffered at the hands of her husband surfaced and landed on me. We went back and forth until I finally managed to break the death-grip on my hair. My vision blurred, nostrils flared. My own mother. How could she stand there and beat on me?

She finally shoved me down, and the tears burst out then. "You're going to school whether you want to or not. That's it. Now get up and clean yourself up."

I didn't move until she left the room. Even then, I got up and flounced on the bed, but I didn't dare lie down again or pull the covers up. I'd been beaten before, far worse. But not by Mama. My insides heaved, doing flips. I couldn't slow my heartbeat and didn't really want to. The anger seethed, growing stronger, pounding against my head.

Fury stomped through me. Nothing new there.

My temper had gotten bad. Sometimes in the middle of a fight, I blanked out. I didn't know what happened until after the fight ended. One time, I got so mad I almost ran over someone with my car. I missed, but only because they moved out of the way.

"I'll show her. I'll get even."

I stomped to the bathroom and washed my face. I might get dressed, but I wasn't going to school, and she couldn't make me—especially from work.

By afternoon, the initial anger subsided, I ran into a friend.

"What's wrong with you?" she asked. "You look like you could beat up a whole gang."

"My mother. You wouldn't believe what she did this morning."

Skipping the part about missing school, the story launched with vivid details. Recounting every word, I stopped only long enough to watch her eyes grow wider. She threw in a few comments. As the story grew, the feelings from the morning returned.

"You should get outta there," she said as the story winded down. "Get away and don't go back—ever."

But where?

I walked for a while and found a lady my mom knew. She had a house behind her home. If I could just convince her I needed a place to stay. Memories of that old lie I used with my aunt popped up. I lied again, saying my stepdad raped me.

Her face tightened. "I'm gonna call CPS. What about your mother? Does she know?"

"No, please don't call them." If she called them, the gig was up. They'd tell her I lied about it before. "They won't do anything, and Mama don't believe me either. None of them believed me before. If you report it, he'll be really pissed off. He'll kill me. I know he will." I forced tears out of my eyes to make my story more believable. "I just need a place to live for a while, but I don't have any money. Please."

"You poor baby. You come stay in my little house as long as you need to, and don't you worry about paying me no rent. C'mon. I'll take you to get your things."

"Oh no, I don't want to trouble you. I got it. He and Mama are both at work. I'll get my stuff and be back in no time."

"Are you sure?"

I nodded. "Thank you so much."

I smiled all the way home. What a sucker. She totally fell for it. I'd convince her later not to tell

Mama.

I hurried, got all my clothes and moved in. No more fighting with Mama, no one to tell me what to do, when to be home or anything else. I was free—except for fear of the lady telling my mother she gave me a place to stay. I tossed and turned, half-waiting for a knock on the door and Mama pulling me home by my hair.

The next day, I slept in until noon or after. When I finally got up, my hands shook. I jumped at every little noise. What if Mama found me? Was I far enough away? I chewed my fingernails, trying to figure out what to do next. I didn't have money, and there wasn't any food. My new ally would feed me, but I wouldn't risk any of her questions. My friends had anything I wanted. Food, booze and even drugs. The thought of getting high calmed my churning stomach. I threw on clothes and walked to the Southside.

Later that night, drunk and high, I started walking back home. Dim streetlights shined on the ground, lighting the way.

A car pulled up beside me, a nice-looking guy in the driver's seat. "Wanna ride?"

"Sure."

From the first minute, he started talking dirty, suggesting things I didn't want to do.

"Stop the car and let me out," I demanded.

He kept driving, pulling me toward him, and

putting his hands all over me.

"Please stop," I pleaded. He laughed—a cackling sound that shimmied up my arms and down my back. He still wouldn't stop.

I jerked away from him, grabbed the door handle, pulled on it and jumped out. The brakes squealed. As I ran away, the engine revved. My foggy head told me run faster. Light surrounded the walk and grass. Heat from the car bore down on me. My feet scrambled, sweat poured from every inch of my body as I tried to move faster. Suddenly, metal hit and I went down. Excruciating pain submerged me as everything went black.

When I woke up, a large cast covered my left leg, lifted in a sling. An IV dripped sweet liquid, numbing the pain. For the next month, the hospital became home. I pretended to have no memory of the incident. Why deal with the police? After all, drunk and high at 16 wasn't gonna look good. So much for freedom.

Mama showed up at the hospital. Every day she came by, assuring the nurses of her love. At least she didn't pull my hair or try to get me out of bed. The perfect picture of a caring mother. I wanted to puke. I hated the idea of going back home. One day of freedom wasn't enough.

After they released me from the hospital, Mama registered me with home school. I ditched the teacher every day. Finally, she stopped coming. Three more times, Mama registered me in a school on the west side of Fort Worth. To the outside world, she seemed perfect, giving me money and trying to keep me in school. For me, it felt like control tactics. She didn't want me to run again.

I had money, Mama made sure. Yet I learned how to shoplift, never considering consequences. Somehow, no one ever caught me. My mom dropped me off at the bus stop, and I hit the back door of the city bus before it pulled away from the curb.

Before long, friends in the club welcomed me back—on crutches. At the door, always lying about my age, I forgot how old I really was. I lied about my age to everyone, not just to get into clubs. I bragged about my experiences of getting high, making up fantastic stories to fit in. A great liar, they believed me. Never feeling much like I belonged at home or school, I found a place where people accepted me. Who cared if what they believed didn't have an ounce of truth. They opened their hearts to me and shared what they had.

At an after-hours club, I met my first pimp. He had all the answers and spent time trying to teach me how to make money. He quickly grew frustrated.

"You're too damn slow. I'll never make a living with you. Get away from me."

That didn't bother me. What did I need with a pimp? He taught well, more than he knew. Working for myself—that's the life. Exciting and loads of money. The taste of living free and on my own tantalized. I breathed in the possibility, dreaming of beautiful clothes and a nice house—nicer than Mama's house and without the beatings. I had it all figured out.

But that's when the drugs came along.

People always want to ask me about my drug problem - I never had a drug problem; I had a self-esteem problem!

Gloria Gaynor

CHAPTER 9

THE AGONY OF DECEIT

At 17, I started taking speed, snorting cocaine or smoking primos every now and then. The first blunt scared me. Thinking it was pure weed, I took a hit with no idea they put cocaine in it. My heart beat incredibly fast—faster and faster—the most intense high I experienced from smoking a joint. No matter what I tried, my heart whizzed like an out of control freight train. It wouldn't slow, and I wondered if it might stop after exploding. But if everyone else took a drag off a primo, I had to do it. Otherwise, they called me names and made fun of me. Whatever they did, I did too.

The days of other people bullying me lived in the past. All I had to do was follow their example and do what they did. Memories of those days with Sheila and her friends lived far back in my brain, only taken out when I wanted to remember why I needed to do something I didn't want to do. I hadn't seen her in years.

Then, one day I was on my way to the bus stop to go visit a friend. Sheila and two of her friends showed up.

"Where you goin'? she asked.

"Just to see a friend."

She grabbed my money. "Walk to your friend's house."

I didn't feel like fighting, especially not with three of them and me by myself. I didn't like getting bullied, but I wasn't stupid. I started walking.

Sheila and her friends rode up on me again. "Get in the car. You gone prostitute for me."

The friends got out and forced me into the backseat. They rode around with me in the car to people they thought had some money. Nobody did, or at least weren't willing to spend it to get with me. Finally, Sheila stopped at a café.

Two men sat in the café. I kept trying to pull

away, but one of the friends gipped my arm so hard it left marks. I looked down, avoiding the men's eyes. My heart beat faster every second. Every fiber of my brain screamed for help, but I kept my mouth shut.

I was for sale so one of the men pulled me off, out of earshot. "You're scared of those girls, aren't you?"

I nodded.

"If you do oral sex on us for free, we'll protect you from them."

Desperation drove me to what I hoped was a good decision. I did just what he asked and then left the café with Sheila and company. The men didn't do anything. Great. Now I'm in for it.

Sheila got in my face as soon as we were outside. "So how much did they give you?"

"None. They didn't' give me nothing'."

"You little liar." She flipped, tried to fight me. "Get back in the car. I'm gone make something off you yet."

I started fighting back, but out of the blue, the two guys appeared. Both had guns and pulled them on her. "Leave her alone. We're taking care of this girl now."

Sheila fumed. For a minute, I thought she was going to jump on one of the men. He cocked his gun. She spit toward him, turned and got in her car with wide-eyed friends jumping in as she pulled away from the curb.

The men pocketed their guns and started to walk away. I stood there for a minute dumfounded. After all I experienced in the past, it surprised me that they kept their word. One of the guys asked if I wanted a ride. I accepted and to my amazement, he took me home. I never saw any of them again, but I learned that I could fight back. For someone like Sheila, my willingness to fight, however I could, didn't work. I was supposed to cower before her, and when I didn't, she flipped.

Before long, another guy came along. We became intimate almost immediately and spent a lot of time with his friends. His crowd always seemed high, totally strung out, but they welcomed me. And they always had a free flow of drugs, everyone sharing with everyone else. No one asked my age, no need for lying or showing an ID. They didn't care about much. I soon learned why.

One day, someone brought heroin. Several of them shot it straight into their veins.

"C'mon. Try some of this, girl. It'll make you feel so good."

If I didn't, what would they think? I wanted to fit in with the crowd around us, so I agreed. But afraid of needles, I chose to snort the dope. It didn't make me feel great. In fact, I hated the way it made me feel. Besides, everyone knew heroin seized you and took control fast. I didn't want any of that.

Life was good with friends who accepted me, and a boyfriend who didn't use me and walk away. Then, all the sex caught up with me. What Mama always said came true. Pregnant at 18. One day I caught my boyfriend smoking some crack. He looked mellow, but still coherent.

"What you smoking?"

"Just a little crack. Wanna hit?"

"Yeah, I'll try some."

Euphoria washed over every inch of my being. I loved the feeling. Peacefulness surrounded me. This was good—for me anyway. The baby—not so much. I still had a sense of doing right, so I smoked it only a few times until the baby boy came. After that, freedom.

Crack. Sweet ecstasy. See I didn't wanna get sprung on it. And I wouldn't. It was all under control. Our baby needed us, so the crack took the edge off the never-ending demands of a newborn. I wanted to do it every now and then. Crack had no control over me. It was okay. Such thoughts.

Every now and then turned into every week. Every week turned into every day.

The addiction dug in, firmly planting its claws throughout my body. Sucking in my mind and leaving me with a lie that I could walk away anytime and never touch crack again. Any time. So convincing. I used every day, but in my brain, I wasn't addicted.

When I got my first apartment, still in Fort Worth, I let anyone come into my house and get high. For about six months, people came and went at the constant party. Drugs came in with different people—people I didn't know. What difference did it make? No one telling me what to do or beating on me.

Then one day, my son got sick. Maybe this wasn't as good as I thought. I had no idea how to take care of a baby. So, I moved back home with my mom to try to get my life on track.

I talked about straightening out my life, how I wanted to do it for my son. Inside I believed myself, but I didn't make an effort. I continued getting high, using my shoplifting skills even at home. The more they complained the more I took, trying to make everything better the only way I knew how. Every time they caught me, I'd promise to change, promise it was the last time. My family grew tired of me stealing from them. Nothing changed from my childhood. They all still wanted to control me, telling me what to do and how to live. I expected them to help me, but they weren't helping. I grew tired of them too. I needed a way out of the situation. I missed the freedom I had before moving back in with them.

Then I found out about low-income housing assistance. I should have known about it. After all, I grew up in the projects. But I never knew how to get help. I didn't say anything to my family, but waited until I got approved. As soon as the approval came through, I moved out. No more following everyone else's rules for me. The taste of freedom refreshed me. Maybe without all of the control, I really could get my head straight.

We stayed in the low-income housing located in downtown Fort Worth. Empowered by having my own place, anything seemed possible. Nothing and no one controlled me. Since I had my own place and rules, I let my son's father live with us. With a place to live and a son in common, he'd stay around. He'd love me and take care of me.

His idea of taking care of me didn't look exactly like I imagined. He always hustled drugs for us. In return, he expected to do what he wanted whenever he wanted. Too much control. He wasn't gonna tell me what to do. Sometimes, I refused to have sex when he wanted it. Ooh, that made him mad—furious at times. He didn't hold back his anger either. He had his way of controlling me.

One night, we both got high. He started kissing on me and running his hands all over my body.

"Leave me alone." I pushed him away. "I just wanna sleep. I'm too tired."

"You ain't turning me down this time." He yanked me toward him. "You give it to me or I'll take it."

He hit me. I tried to get away. He pulled me back and hit me again. I kicked at him and tried to run. Adrenaline coursing through both of our veins, we started fighting. I wasn't strong enough to last for long. The blows connected one after the other until I gave up and went down. Then his foot found my ribcage several times. After a while, he stopped and stormed out of the room. The pain left me in a fog, unable to move. I knew I should run, but the thought of leaving him terrified me. So I stayed.

The beatings continued over time, usually brought on by my own stubbornness and unwillingness to bend to his control over me. The drugs affected my judgement, giving me a boldness to fight, the belief I could win. But he always overpowered and left me writhing in pain and fear.

He sold drugs for someone—I never knew who. I didn't want to know. He didn't use the money to take care of us though. He took the money and smoked it up. Finally, he left and moved to another side of town. Where was his love? Brokenhearted and defeated yet again, I gave up the housing assistance. Packing up my son, I moved back home with Mama. I hated the idea, but didn't know where else to go. I couldn't make it without my man.

Still addicted to drugs, I kept seeing this same guy. He supplied drugs and sex, both cravings I couldn't deny. Before long, I became pregnant again. This time I had a baby girl. Surely having two kids together would make this man love me. We moved in together again. Like the proverbial moth to a flame, my life was a cliché. This time around, we lived in a low-income apartment on the east side of Fort Worth. Rent cost only $35.00 a month, and even then, we had a hard time paying it. The fantasy of happily-ever-after ended abruptly within days, if it ever existed at all. We kept getting high. The beatings had gotten out of control, but so had my drug addiction. I endured his fists and feet to get what I desperately wanted. I did whatever it took to pay for drugs.

I sold all of my daughter's diapers. When she wet, I used a shirt or a towel as a diaper. I sold all my food stamps. I only went to WIC for the baby formula. I sold my baby daughter's milk. I didn't bathe nor comb my hair. I walked around with a wool winter cap on my head for a long time. I treated my baby girl the same way. She went for days without a bath. When I didn't eat, neither did she. Part of me hated the truth of the terrible life handed to her. But then the drugs dimmed the shame and guilt.

Anyone could come in my house to get high or do whatever he or she wanted to do. When my daughter was only 6 months old, I got pregnant again. During the first two pregnancies, I backed off from drugs some, at least from crack. But this time I couldn't. For the whole pregnancy, I smoked crack—never went to the doctor or worried much about the coming baby.

Crack dug its talons deep in my veins, controlling me more than any person ever did. Unable to break the drug's hold, I surrendered to the intoxicating effect, letting it wash away my sense of right and wrong. Nothing mattered as long as I stayed high. But eventually, I came down and sometimes reality smacked me in the face. Shame beat me up during those moments. No one had to tell me drugs weren't good for my unborn child. I wanted to change, straighten myself up.

Some of my friends went to a small family church. I went with them and joined. The people there accepted me. Most of the time when I went to church, I scurried out the door as soon as they said the final amen—sometimes before. I went straight home and got high. Some Sundays throughout the service, guilt washed over me. I thought about my children and the baby inside me, thinking I needed to live better for them. Deep inside, my conscience screamed at me. How could I make such a mess and drag my children through it all with me? People in and out with drugs, having sex and the beatings—they saw it all. Maybe going to church would make it all better. I kept details about my life outside of church a secret, hidden from anyone there— especially my friends. Looking back, they probably knew, but didn't judge me. They didn't need to. I did enough judging of myself, allowing shame to point a finger and poke my heart. At the end of the time, I still left church, running to drugs so I could forget how terrible of a person I somehow became.

How did I get so awful? "I can quit using anytime," I lied to myself. "When and if I want to quit, I will."

All of the self-deceit about controlling drugs so I didn't get addicted was a joke. My addiction clung to me like thorny vines ripping at the fabric of my body and soul. Still, I convinced myself everything was okay. It really wasn't, and I knew it. But as long as the drugs kept coming, I didn't worry about any of that.

Toward the end of my pregnancy, my children's dad made a huge mistake. He had some guy's drugs and smoked them all instead of holding or selling them. Scared, he ran off. I didn't realize it then, but it was the best thing that ever happened to me. With him gone, the beatings stopped.

Before long, he denied having any children. Especially when a new girlfriend came along, he sure didn't want to admit we had children together. I felt like they were trick babies, conceived by molestation and certainly not in love. I never told my kids anything bad about him or his family. But I kept my distance. I built a wall around us. If he wanted to see the kids, he knew where my mom stayed.

High on crack, I managed to get myself to the hospital when labor pains started. I literally passed out during the hours of being in labor. The next day, when I finally came back to myself, the nurse brought my new son to me. He weighed six pounds and fifteen ounces.

The doctor came in and told me he was addicted to crack. How could he be addicted to crack? He was just a baby. Besides, I wasn't addicted, so he sure couldn't be. They were wrong. Everything about him seemed normal— everything other than him crying more than my other babies did. They released both of us the next day. Convinced all was well, we went home.

And then the call came.

And you, fathers, do not provoke your children to wrath, but bring them up in the training and admonition of the Lord.

Apostle Paul (Ephesians 6:4, NKJV)

CHAPTER 10

CPS

"I'm with CPS and saw your son in the hospital," she said.

The coldness of her voice sent ice through my veins. Good thing she was on the phone and not at my house.

I countered with a light-hearted answer. "He's a cute little guy isn't he?"

She ignored the comment. "He's a crack baby. Do you know what that means?"

Two could play this game. I kept my mouth

shut.

"He could have died. For now, he seems stable. But his life won't be easy. You sentenced him to mental retardation. At best, he'll be a slow learner. Your crack addiction, passed on to your son destroyed his future."

I imagined the glare in her eyes, smoldering like a fire and ready to burst into huge flames at any second. She continued for several minutes, passing judgement on me, telling me what a mess I made. Every word pricked my heart, but instead of feeling sorry, anger rose, bubbling, waiting for a chance to lash out at her. Finally, she took a breath.

"I'm not addicted to crack, and my baby is fine," I shouted. "He's small, but no more than my other babies were. He's good. You'll see."

For a few seconds, she didn't respond. A deep inhale came across the line, and then blew out. "Regardless of what you think, CPS just became your worst nightmare. We can't allow you to keep your baby. And we're picking up your other children as well."

"No!"

The call ended abruptly. Rage catapulted me across the room. I had a short time to get out of there, but where would I go? They'd find me. A sudden rush of sorrow broke out as loud sobs and drove me to sit down. How could they take my kids? But they did.

Mama came through for once. They allowed her to take custody of all three of my babies. I'd show them. Crack didn't have control over me. And my son wasn't retarded. I refused to believe anything they said. The doctors and nurses told me the same thing, their words beating me down, pouring guilt over my head. Dark depression fell around me, locking me into fits of crying followed by intense anger, and the ever-deepening longing for just one hit. I needed that one hit to escape the guilt tormenting me and fear they might be right about my son.

With CPS involved, I moved back home with my mom. I hated every minute of being in the house with her. She constantly reminded me about my inability to be a good mother to my kids. But they were wrong about my son. He developed normally. Still Mama poured on the criticism. Every morning I woke to her accusations, and at some point, I had to agree. I hadn't treated my kids well. I wasn't a great mother—not even a particularly good one. Guilt filled my mind, ravishing my heart until I wanted to cry. But crying did no good and Mama made sure shame followed me every waking minute.

Her words played repeatedly in my head. Only one thing silenced them—drugs.

I did anything to supply my habit and get

release from Mama's mental bullets. Having sex paid well enough to get what I needed. It didn't matter if the tricks were men or women. As long as they paid, that's all that mattered.

I always had an excuse to leave my children on my mom. Sometimes I lied, telling her "I be right back. I'm going to the corner store."

Two or three days later, I might get back home. During those days I smoked crack, prostituted myself, performed bi-sexual acts or anything it took to get high. At moments where my conscience piped up with convicting thoughts, I quickly silenced it with a little crack— or a lot.

CPS insisted I attend NA/AA meetings and other classes. No problem. With all the other talents and skills, lying came easy.

"Are you using?"

"No, no. I ain't getting' high no more."

They didn't believe me. The conversations went on for a while, but sooner or later, one of them said, "Let's do a quick test. For your records."

I cringed. How did they know? Every time, the drug test came back dirty. The guilt pricked at my heart, tears stinging my eyes. Why did I keep getting high, especially when I knew they'd test me and find out? I didn't want to be a drug addict. I wanted my kids back, to be a good mom. So in shame, I enrolled in a drug treatment center, vowing to get better. Sixteen times in a single year, I repeated the cycle.

One day, I headed out of the house, hell bent on getting high. On my way, a lady stopped me.

"Can I pray for you?" she asked.

I shrugged my shoulders. "Okay. Not sure what good it will do, but yeah, go ahead."

The words went over my head, most of them falling helplessly to the ground. Who was the God she prayed to? At one time, He seemed real enough, but what did He do for me? He certainly didn't keep me from the drugs. But every time I headed for the drug house, that woman stood in my path. Every time, she asked to pray for me, and I relented. And every time, the emotions tried to get the best of me, but the desire for drugs dug its claws in deeper.

When dope called me, I did anything to get it. I mean any and every thing. As I went out street walking, men would stop me to have sex with them for drugs or some small change. Five or ten dollars, sometimes less. That represented the value I placed on myself. Sometimes they didn't have any money, and they just took advantage of me, helping themselves to free sex.

One night, I walked home. As I passed a guy talking on a pay phone, he reached out and stopped me.

"Hey, Baby. You wanna get high? You want some crack?"

"Sure." Knowing he didn't expect to give it to me for nothing, I climbed into the car with him.

"I have to pick up my friend. He's got the stuff."

"No problem." I sat back anticipating the high.

After his friend got in with us, he drove to this house. I willingly went inside with the two men, every nerve tingling, relishing the moment when we soared to an ecstatic stupor. Instead, one of the guys pulled out a gun.

"Get on your knees and suck me," he demanded as he undid his pants.

I didn't argue. I figured that was my price for crack. The gun made me a bit uncomfortable, but it wasn't the first time I saw one. Laughter drifted over the room as they both watched.

The other one pushed me down, yanking at my clothes. He flipped me over and pushed himself in my anus. "If you get any s___ on me, you'll lick it off, and then I'll kill you."

A scream rose in my throat, but I couldn't release it. I lay still praying for God to keep him clean. Sweat covered my body while I tried to control the trembling and failed miserably. Oh God, don't let them kill me. Don't let them kill me.

Terror gripped me, paralyzing my legs and

arms. When he finished they slapped me around, threatening me more.

"You still want some crack?"

"No. I just wanna go home. Please. I won't tell anyone. Just let me go."

They both laughed and hit me some more. Finally, they led me out to the car and put me in the trunk.

Oh God, they're going to kill me. They're gonna take me somewhere, shoot me and dump my body. I'll never see my babies again. They'll grow up without a mama.

The car moved for what seemed like hours. Bumps in the road bounced me around, sometimes upward so my head hit the top of the trunk. Where was God? Was the woman from the street still praying for me?

"God, help me," I shouted. Prayer burst out of my mouth, words filling the small space and tumbling back over me.

"Shut up you stupid b…" A verbal assault commenced, vile words fired at me like missiles hitting their target and filling me with terror.

I kept praying, but God didn't answer. In that moment, I doubted His existence more than ever before. I gave up on God long before that night, but in the trunk, I decided I was right. In all the bad I'd done, surely I didn't deserve this ending to my life. If there was a God, why would He let this happen? No longer able to hold back the tears, I sobbed and cried out for mercy from a being that I denied existed.

Eventually, the car stopped. This was it. The trunk popped open.

"Get out!"

Somehow, I climbed out of the trunk. They slammed it shut. I closed my eyes, waiting for the pop of the gun and searing pain. Would I see it coming, or would they shoot me in the back? A minute later, the tires screeched and gravel pounded against my legs. Slowly my eyes opened. No car. I collapsed to the ground.

After a few minutes, I pushed myself up and started walking. I caught sight of a sign with a clock counting the early morning. 3:00 a.m. Trembling, I forced one foot in front of the other. A car approached.

"Need a ride?"

The man looked nice enough, but I wasn't willing to take a chance. "No. I'm fine." I trembled all over. My gut tied itself in knots.

He drove away, but within minutes, he came back around, pulling up close to me. "Are you sure you don't want a ride? You look pretty beat up."

My legs felt like gelatin. Could I trust this man? Weariness rolled over me. "Okay."

Safe in his car, words spilled out. Sobs

overtook me again as I told the stranger what happened that night. He pulled the car over, comforting, holding, kissing me. Within minutes, we entered the back seat and had sex. He tossed ten dollars my way and dropped me off at the dope house.

Getting high, I shared the story again with my friends. A few nods, but no one cared. Most didn't even acknowledge me. For the first time, I wanted to be home, safe with Mama and my children. The initial high evened out. As morning approached, I left the dope house, walking toward home.

Another stranger picked me up. He promised money for sex. With my judgement impaired, I accepted. He drove to the park and took advantage of me. He left me there and didn't bother to pay. Used again. How could so much happen to me in one night? Far from home, I headed out again and opened the door just before daylight.

The first time I headed back to the dope house, the praying woman met me as if she waited just for me. Again, she wanted to pray. The offering meant nothing, or so I thought. But after a while, her words irritated me, doubts of a benevolent God mixing with the guilt and shame Mama poured over my head. So, I tried to go a different direction and avoid the woman. It was like she knew which street I took, and she ended up right there.

One day, we crossed paths yet again. She gave me a green prayer cloth. "Keep this in your bra."

"What?"

"Just keep it there. I'm still praying for you."

I walked away shaking my head. "Can't I even enjoy my high I get tripping and skitzing?"

CPS prepared to close my case. A month to go, they gave Mama partial custody. I questioned their wisdom. The classes and programs helped me. I learned things, even if they didn't keep me from going back to drugs.

Six months after they closed my case, I called the caseworker, begging her to reopen my case. They gave me a lifeline for help and sanity, although I dismissed it again as guilt. Desperate and even filled with doubt about His existence, I sometimes asked God to let the police take me to jail. Now how insane is that?

Thoughts of suicide drifted in and out of my head. One time I was in drug treatment with depression attached. A deep hole sat below me, ready to reach up and drag me in so deep I'd never climb out. I left the treatment center with anti-depressants, but no less depressed than when I entered. I didn't see a way out, and the thought drove me closer to the hole.

A friend invited me to a revival. For some

reason, I agreed. She prayed over me during the service.

Her sweet, soft voice touched a place in my soul no one else seemed able to reach. "God heals depression."

"How?"

"Just believe, ask, and He will heal you."

Why should I believe? Did He even exist? But her eyes glistened in the low light, filled with assurance of her faith.

Nothing else had worked for me. Nothing. Maybe I should try it.

"I believe. God, please heal me."

After that day, I never took the medication again. But the addiction to drugs didn't let go. It held as tight as ever.

Behold, I stand at the door and knock. If anyone hears my voice and opens the door, I will come in to him and eat with him, and he with me.

Jesus Christ

CHAPTER 11
SUNDAY, SEPTEMBER 19, 1994

For a year and eight months, CPS kept the case open, watching out for my kids. It didn't change anything. Drugs called with the strength of ten giant monsters, always pulling me to them.

I had been at the crack house for a day or two. My brother and his wife showed up and knocked on the door. My mother and children waited in the car.

Mama had a message for me. "I know what you're doing. I wish you had enough respect to come home and get your kids."

Something came over me. I needed to go and see my kids. I did leave them while I chased after drugs. A part of me wanted to get myself together and the other half loved the way I lived. Was it so bad to leave them out of the drug scene? Maybe not, but at the same time, they were my kids.

I went home with everyone else. Old feelings of guilt and shame bombarded me. I never took care of my kids. I left them for days at a time, and even after coming back, I didn't treat them well. They barely knew me.

Something had to change.

I called a lady from narcotics anonymous.

"I want to change for the sake of my kids," I confessed. "But the drugs help me escape everything bad in my life. What can I do? How can I beat this thing?"

This lady didn't play around. She gave it to me straight. "If you're sincere about staying clean, eat something, take a bath and get on your knees. Tell God you wanna surrender but you don't know how."

Tasteless food squeezed down past a lump. The water washed away days of filth and pain. Then literally, on my knees, I cried out to God. I no longer doubted His existence. For the first time, responsibility for all the bad behaviors with drugs and my kids fell on my shoulders, pushing down and overwhelming me. Then suddenly, God took them from me, forgiving me. Freshness descended, removing the guilt and shame. Breathing deeply, warmth spread over every bit of my body. Any traces of drugs ran away. Clarity and peace took over my senses, stronger than the influence of any amount of drugs I ever did.

Ever since that day, getting high lost its priority. When God took the drugs away, He took away everything that broke me down— prostitution, bi-sexual and whatever attracted me to drugs. For that, I give God all the glory.

A fresh start emerged, with nothing stopping me. A week later, I enrolled in a beauty and barber college. I found other positive things to do such as going to church and NA meetings-- anything to better myself.

But coming to Jesus didn't make life perfect. The years of abuse and neglect left holes trust couldn't fill. Even though I never doubted God's forgiveness, finding it from people came harder.

I still wanted love, went looking for it. Maybe I needed someone to rescue me, to help me pursue this new life. I sure wanted a man to protect me from my brother and people like him. And I found it in a new boyfriend.

After being clean for a year, I wanted to have

another baby, this time without drugs anywhere near or thinking that could keep a man or make him love me. Soon after that, I got pregnant. When I told Mama, she glared at me, upset because I was pregnant with my fourth child at the age of 26.

Her jaw tightened and eyes narrowed. Strangled anger leaked through her calm voice. "You're outta here. Pack your stuff and take your kids with you."

"But this is my house."

"You don't deserve this house, and I've stayed here more than you ever did. Get out."

Where would I go? Pregnant with three children. She couldn't throw me out. The fight continued until the police showed up. They made me leave my house, taking the children and me to a shelter.

I was homeless even though I owned the house where Mama lived.

I stayed in the shelter with my kids. I hated it and couldn't keep up with the duties they assigned because I was sick. They put us out after one week.

One of my friends had a dope house. Why not take my children and stay there? At least we wouldn't be living on the street. For a week, we did. It wasn't the best place to have my babies, but I didn't know what else to do. I applied for housing.

Then, as suddenly as Mama put me out, she allowed us to come back and stay. But for how long?

My brother didn't want my mom to let me and the children move back in, but she didn't listen to him. I went to a food bank, trying to be a good mother and provide food for us.

One day my brother came over. "What's all this?"

"I went to a food bank. I need to finish this course so I can get a good job. Then I'll be able to buy food."

"Get a job now. This garbage is worthless, barely fit for a dog. How can you eat this junk or give it to the kids?" He opened a can and poured the contents in the dog bowl. The dog, of course, lapped it up.

Tremors shook me. Heat rose and grabbed my face. "What are you doing?"

I reached for the other cans he removed from the cabinet. He held them high. I clawed at him, but he pushed me down. I wanted to fight him, but my strength collapsed on the floor beside me. He took the food, fed more to the dog and whisked the rest away.

As he walked out, he glanced back, his eyes flashing. "I'm saving you from yourself. You'll thank me someday."

I pulled in my knees and wept. How could he be so cruel, taking food from my kids? I changed, but he still treated me like an addicted, bad mother. Why did he want to punish me instead of helping? His rejection left a deep mark on my soul. Why did God let this happen?

Two weeks later, my low-income housing came through. I packed up my children and moved, leaving my mother in the home I owned.

I shifted from the beauty and barber college, and then six months later I got my first job working for the county hospital. Finally, life looked better. Only six months, but I had a place for my children and me to live and a good job so I could take care of them. I continued to stay clean from drugs.

I made it through the first leg of my journey. The world brightened. I faced consequences from the past, yet succeeded in moving forward to a good life.

But God wasn't finished with me yet.

> The times may have changed, but the people are still the same. We're still looking for love, and that will always be our struggle as human beings.

Halle Berry

CHAPTER 12
OLD ISSUES RISING

After a while, narcotics anonymous got boring. So on payday I dolled up and headed to the club. I wanted love and a daddy for my children. I just couldn't stand being lonely. I felt like the R&B singer, Betty Wright. Having a piece of a man is better than having no man at all. Or Natalie Cole—I catching hell living here alone. Originally, I did anything to try to keep a man, but so far that wasn't working too great.

I never liked guys if they never went through

nothing. Pimps, Playz, hustlers, gang bangers. I tried dating Bloodz, but their swag was too slow. I had to go back to my main thang, the CRIPS. I had to have 'em.

On payday, I thought if I paid Thim or gave him some good sex, that would keep him around, and he would love me.

See I was also a daredevil. If I found out he had another woman, I dared her to tell me I couldn't have him. I wasn't giving up messing with him until he and I got ready. Didn't realize I was making myself look bad. He only came around when it got close to getting paid again. Then he's gone on. But as long as he came around, he must love me. A warped mentality of love controlled my actions.

When one left, I said, "If he don't want me, I will get with somebody else." That's how I always ended relationships, drifting from one to the next as soon as possible. Never a chance to learn or love myself. And that was my biggest problem.

I didn't love me.

Life went on this way, not realizing this constant changing of "love" relationships represented a form of low self-esteem.

Then, in 2002, I met a man. Oh my goodness. I finally met someone. Someone different. He wasn't the same as all the others I knew. He really loved me. I didn't have to buy him with my money. I didn't have to give him sex or a child to keep him. I finally met someone good—we called him Bigg Daddy.

He was the best man I ever met. I've been involved with a lot of guys. I thought I was in love with others, or I was always trying to find a dad or a family for my children. Bad way to look at life. It may sound crazy, but I fell hard for this man. I was grown with children when we met— how silly to swoon over him. But Bigg Daddy was my first true love. We dated for more than 10 years. I never worried about him cheating on me. We lived in a fairytale world. Not perfect, but close. Love filled my home. He treated my kids like they belonged to him. "We have a lifetime contract," he said.

Everything was good—except for one big problem. He got addicted to drugs. I finally knew how others felt when they had to deal with me being an addict. He was never a bad person. He was simply lost. Having broken free from that life, I couldn't deal with it. No desire to go back, his addiction reminded me of the awful place I lived for so many years. The only thing keeping us from a beautiful life together forever and he didn't want to give it up. Our situation became so overwhelming he moved out of town.

Brokenhearted and still hating the loneliness of being single, I moved on to another relationship.

I grew tired of waiting on Bigg Daddy. I had no idea when or if he'd come back. And if he did, would he give up the drugs?

I tried clubbing again and met this man. I didn't want him. He wasn't a good man. I was just doing something to keep from being lonely. I still loved me some Bigg Daddy. While I tried to hurt Bigg Daddy, I got hurt the worst.

User always. Get used. He stole my car, rent money. This guy stole everything from me, leaving behind all his clothes and personal information. I started seeing this path of what I considered love, didn't work. Too many men over the years and the only one close to stability had an issue too big for us to ignore. Maybe, just maybe, God had a better way.

And while I'm going thru all this hell, Bigg Daddy came back to town. Two years of living out of the state, and all of the sudden he returned. I wanted Bigg Daddy back, but that wasn't best for my children or me. A seed of self-respect implanted in my heart. The old mentality about love slowly faded. I'd been taken advantage of one too many times. Even though I had a hard time letting him go, I had to learn a new way. When you trust God to bless you with something like a husband or a wife, He gotta prepare you to receive it. I never stayed with anyone long because I chose bad. Quite frankly, I wasn't prepared to receive a godly man. I needed time to let God get me ready.

Today, Bigg Daddy and I are still friends no matter what. He was my very first true love. A single thought of him, the mention of his name, made my heart flutter. Despite all of our struggles or situation, he and his family always treated me well. Often he and I argued. In the middle of our argument, someone else attacked him. Not.

"That's my Bigg Daddy. If you got a problem with him take it up with me." I even disrespected his mother at times. I didn't care if he was right or wrong. The other person might have said the same thing I spoke over him. None of that mattered. When someone came against this man, the bear in me came alive. It reached out and held them by the throat, protecting the man I loved. Protecting the only man who loved me back.

As I looked deep in myself with open eyes, I faced truth about my warped ideas of love. If I gave a man money, somehow that made him stay. But he always found a way to leave me for someone else that could give him more.

The rejection and abandonment left me feeling like nothing I did was ever enough. Did any of those men really love me? I came to grips with truth—money can't buy love. The idea conjured from my childhood wasn't any better than the things I saw and hated in my mother.

Out from under the curse of stew head syndrome, the truth soaked my wounded heart and mind. The old mindset drifted away, a slow, sometimes painful journey, until death took it and set me free to learn about real love.

Today I feel good waking up, being married to the body of Christ, being a tither, and obedient to whatever God wants me to do. If God tells me jump I just do. I get to ask Him any question without fear He will never leave, cheat on me or pummel me with His fist. He accepts me just as I am.

I feel so good loving somebody, knowing that somebody actually loves me back with a love that is completely without conditions. This love is what my heart always wanted, searched for in men. This love comes from only one being—and that's God.

The strong desire for sex no longer exists. I understand sex is not the same as love. For the last eight years, I keep walking in freedom from sex. Someday, God may give me a husband. I hope so. But for now, He is the only love I need.

I'm a born-again Christian, but that's not the coat that I wear. It's just how my heart's been changed.

Tony Vincent

CHAPTER 13
NEW CREATION

Second Corinthians 5:17 says, "Therefore, if anyone is in Christ, he is a new creation; old things have passed away; behold, all things have become new." (NKJV)

I watched Mama deal with what others thought of her. Don't know how she overcame it or what she did, but I prayed and God delivered me. "Therefore I say to you, whatever things you ask when you pray, believe that you receive them, and you will have them." (Mark 11:24, NKJV)

During that time, I feared having sex. AIDs floated around like crazy. Up to that time in my life, God spared me from contracting HIV. I decided to give all of my sexuality to God, to wait on Him and do things the way He desired. I'd been with so many people, and I wanted a husband. But I had to allow God to upgrade me. He had to teach me how to be a wife. Until that time when I am married, no more sex for me.

I watched my son grow. So many people told me he was going to be retarded or slow because of the crack I used. He got his diploma a year early. When I saw a CPS worker 13 years later, I rejoiced in telling her of his success.

At one time, if a person asked me for $100, I would break my neck to give it to them. Yet, if I went to a discount store and saw a five-dollar blouse, that was too much to spend on myself. Now, I never think anything is too much to spend on myself. I love going shopping for me. While I may not buy something because I don't have the money, I don't see myself as not deserving what I want in spite of the cost.

In the past, I couldn't tell you what I like to do for fun. Now I can tell you. Skating, plays, going out to eat, bowling… The world stands before me with so many fun opportunities. Even when money gets tight, I can always find something I enjoy.

I am a new creature, and in that state I see wonder in each day. Life isn't always easy. God never promises a life without trials. But through His eyes and with His presence, the world takes on new beauty. Every day brings new hope and dreams. Everything looks different. The old is gone, and all things appear fresh for me. In Christ, I look back—not with longing to be in those places, but to learn and then share what He shows me with others.

I am a new creation in Jesus.

God accepted me without telling me to change myself. But then He undertook the task of changing me into the woman He planned for me from the start. I learned to stop trying to figure out everyone else and focus on me.

And then my daddy reappeared, and I had to look at myself in relationship to him.

The human father has to be confronted and recognized as human, as man who created a child and then, by his absence, left the child fatherless and then Godless.

Anais Nin

CHAPTER 14
DADDY'S LITTLE GIRL

Relationship with my dad was very weird to me. I never had a relationship with him. I really didn't know him, but knew of him. Many times, I wanted to visit him. I asked my mother to take me. Sometimes she answered, "I'm your daddy." Other times she said, "You ain't got no daddy." The words stung every time, and I didn't understand why she didn't want me to see him.

I knew some of my dad's family, but not everybody. His sisters were evangelists. We had no choice but to learn about God, but with all the drama going on at home with Mama, it caused division between us.

My last name always created a source of pain for me. My brothers and I had different dads, but I went by their dad's last name. For years, I was confused. People teased me, tortured me about my last name. I suffered at home, school or wherever I went. For a long time, some family members tried to make me feel like my mom didn't know who my dad was. Some people still say she doesn't.

I always asked Mama, "Why didn't you give me my daddy's last name? Can't you change it to his last name?"

Her biting words dug into my heart. "You ain't got no daddy, and when you get grown you'll get married and change your last name then.

"But you gave JR his dad's last name and I can't have mine?"

"Girl, shut up. I don't want to talk about it no more."

My stepdad stood nearby. She said, "Teresa, there's your daddy."

He responded with his usual harshness. "I AIN'T your daddy."

Once again my head hung, confusion swarming over me. Rejected, unloved—I didn't know who I was. If my daddy didn't want me, even acknowledge me, how could anyone else? Including myself.

My dad had an auto mechanic shop on the south side of Fort Worth. When I asked my mother to see him, she often responded, "He ain't got nothing to give you no way."

Every time I called his shop or stopped by, he had someone tell me, "He's not around."

Even with all of that, I used to love telling people who my dad was. It made me feel like he was a celebrity, and that made me somebody important. His reputation was awesome. Nobody said anything negative about him. One lady in particular bragged about how good of a man he was to her and her family. My heart hurt at her constant bragging. He never treated me like that, never acknowledged my existence. How could he be so wonderful to this woman and care so little about me?

Somehow, I had to find gratitude for this man. Desperate for some kind of reconciliation, I had no idea how to make it happen.

In 2003, my dad became a resident in a nursing home. In 2006, I became an employee at that same nursing home. Every time payday came around, he sat outside waiting for me to pass him. He always said, "Let me hold something. I bought your first car and bicycle."

Father's Day rolled around. I went to work

and took him a Father's Day card.

He barely looked at the card. "Is that all you think of me is a card? After everything I done for you?"

His words stung like a wasp on steroids, reaching all the way to my tender heart. Tears burned. I didn't try to keep them from pouring out. I saw my mother standing right there beside me, her voice saying, "All he gone do is lie. He ain't gone give you nothing."

Did he really give me a bike or a car? Did he ever give me anything? Years of disappointment and anger rose in my belly, steaming and bubbling to a full boil. Rage rose, threatening to spill over and unleash itself on this man I so desperately wanted to hurt as much as he hurt me.

As much as I wanted to love my daddy, reality flooded me. My heart hated him. The thought of seeing him one more day turned my stomach. Paydays flashed before me, the many times he wanted money from me, trying to convince me he did something that made him deserve it. All lies. I couldn't stand it. I couldn't stand him. I hated him.

Within days, I quit my job.

A year later, it felt like God was tugging on me to go back to work with him. God, what? I can't do it. I can't take the pain again. He can't hurt me if I don't see him. Go back. I kept hearing the same thing. It's too hard. I can't.

But I did.

"I just won't bother him," I decided. I couldn't not visit him though.

Every time I went to his room, he always told me, "Go on up the hall. I will see you later."

Every time, the stinger hit its mark. In His miraculous way, God touched those bites and took away the pain.

One day, God spoke to me and said, "You're not the one your dad wants to see."

He wanted to see those people he actually took care of. But I was the one there. To some level, God repaired the relationship. It wasn't exactly what I wanted, not nearly enough, but it was something.

I knew when he was getting ready to pass away. God gave me a vision. There would come a day when I got to work, his bed would be stripped and he would be gone. Two months after that vision, I went to work. His bed was stripped. During my days off, they rushed him to the hospital. I immediately stopped working there. My daddy wouldn't be coming back.

On August 1, 2007, I received a house visit from an ex-coworker to let me know my dad had passed.

Wow. Despite of what he did or didn't do for

me, he's still my dad. I thank God for a chance to be a part of his life before he passed away. I truly thank God for the unity we gained in those short months before his death. A little unity is better than having none at all.

Before he passed away, he informed me that he had 17 daughters. I never was a social media person. Yet, in 2014, I found a lot of my family I never even knew existed. Then we had a family meet and greet. I still didn't know everyone, but it felt good to connect with my own biological family.

All my life, I heard all types of wild and crazy stories from others. As a child, I never understood why sadness clung to me. The stories left me in depression at a young age. Even though my last name is Tarpley, I am a carpenter. First and foremost, I am a child of God. I learned from others' mistakes. Be careful what you do. Your actions affect everyone around you. I came to grips that whatever happened will not stop me from moving forward.

The old stories came back recently. In 2014, I met a young man who told me my mom didn't know who my dad was. Immediately, all the old spirit of confusion and frustration arose. I had to pray and ask God to heal me from the frustration and confusion of others, deliver me from people and reveal the truth.

But I say to you, love your enemies, bless those who curse you, do good to those who hate you, and pray for those who spitefully use you and persecute you

Jesus Christ (Matthew 5:44, NKJV)

CHAPTER 15
WHAT'S UP WITH MAMA?

In 2010, Mama was diagnosed with dementia, high blood pressure and high cholesterol. I immediately stepped in and became her caregiver. Wow, what a job.

In 2011, God started speaking to me about principles of forgiveness. I didn't understand what He meant.

Me and my big mouth.

I just had to ask God what He meant. Next thing I know, both of my sons went to jail and there wasn't anyone around but Mama and me. In the process of deep cleaning her house, I found a letter from a state attorney.

I read the letter in disbelief. How could she? But the letter made it clear. She went behind my back, attempting to have my name removed as owner of the house. I never knew.

When Glen died, there was a trust left for maybe $69,000. I couldn't receive any of the money until I turned 18. Mama always told me not to tell anyone about the money. For years, I watched her go through all of the abuse from her husband, all the while saying she only wanted money. So I started telling men about the trust fund, thinking or doing anything to hold on to them. It never happened. Like everything else I tried in order to keep a man, it never worked.

So when my 18th birthday came, Mama still lived with my stepfather. She wanted a place to stay. So got a house for her. The only thing she gave me out of the money was maybe $300 if that much.

Even when I wasn't living with Mama, she would call and tell me, "When you get your income tax, you need to pay taxes on the house. You never know when you might have to come back home. I often wondered, "Why should I? I don't even live in that house."

My mom tried to pick and choose my

company, even though she lived in my house. Who was she to run my life and determine who could come to my house? Her control in my own home caused arguments many times, leaving even more bad feelings between us.

One day, a bank statement came in the mail. My trust fund had money I knew nothing about. So I went to the bank and withdrew $500. My mother and brother, JR, had a huge problem with it. I didn't see anything wrong with taking money from my bank account.

As I studied the letter, all of these things raced across my thoughts. I remembered when I owned a home, but found myself homeless with three children, pregnant and then on housing assistance. Waves of anger gushed over me, crushing me against rocks of bitterness and sorrow.

I hated her.

I didn't want to, knew I shouldn't, but I did.

Everything she ever did to me started coming back up. It hurt so bad I really didn't know what to do. How could I possibly forgive her? Again, God asked me to do something that seemed impossible. Again, I cried, "It's too hard. I can't."

It wouldn't do any good to ask her about it because of her mental state. I tried talking to other people about the letter, but that was a bad choice. The more I talked about it, the angrier I grew.

Eventually I stopped talking to other people and prayed instead.

"I want to forgive her, but I don't know how."

In His faithfulness, God taught me. Now we have a mother and daughter relationship. I asked her to forgive me for everything I did to hurt her, and I voiced forgiveness for everything she did to me or didn't do for me.

I tell you, when people mistreat you, it is not easy to forgive. I didn't know hatred was in me for so many years. It simmered on the back burner. Mark 11:25-26 says, "And whenever you stand praying, if you have anything against anyone, forgive him, that your Father in heaven may also forgive you your trespasses. But if you do not forgive, neither will your Father in heaven forgive your trespasses."

I can't imagine asking God to forgive me for all my sins and He respond, "No. Why should I? You don't forgive."

If He forgives all the stuff I did, how can I not forgive even the terrible things done to me?

Have you ever been in a relationship with a man or a woman? You wanted them so bad but everybody pushes you away from them and you get the point. When you say the hell with it, 20 years later they come back all used up, stink nasty, broke down like an old shotgun.

In 2012, I had a chance to get my house back after all I went through. The house was like a longed-for relationship, horrible. It would have cost millions to repair that house. Besides, I lost all interest in it. I found out my mother fell thousands of dollars behind on her medical insurance. I had a choice to keep the house and repair it, or sell it. Even though people questioned my wisdom, I chose to sell, making sure I could cover Mama's insurance.

You have to be careful how you treat people. Someday, you might have to depend on the very one you mistreated. Despite what Mama did or didn't do to or for me, I thank God for allowing me to be obedient and for teaching me how to forgive those who hurt and wronged me. That's my daily prayer. Lord, search me and cast out any unforgiveness in me. Lord, teach me how to honor my mother and father, so that my days on earth can be longer even though my dad is dead. My mom is still alive. It's a blessing to be a part of her life.

In January 2014, my mother was rushed to the county hospital. The social worker asked about my uncle. I told her he was deceased. Then she asked about my brother. I told her he's not around. I talked to my brother one time during the whole time she was in the hospital. He said he was coming to the hospital, but never came or answered the phone call until the day before they released her. Then he offered reasons he didn't come or answer his phone. He had a bad headache or toothache.

Anger started bubbling up again, but God spoke and said, "Pray and ask me to connect you to the right people and teach you how to receive them." I chose to obey.

Because of connecting myself to my 83-year-old Mama, I'm still her caregiver. She always accuses me of stealing her house, money and car. Nevertheless, it is a pleasure to be a part of her life. Of course, at times I wanted to give up. But quitters never win and winners never quit. I hold fast to scripture. "Honor your father and your mother, that your days may be long upon the land which the Lord your God is giving you." (Exodus 20:12, NKJV)

This is the first time in my whole life that Mama and I actually get along without arguing or without her trying to take advantage of me. It is truly a blessing to enjoy all the fun and laughter with her regardless of our past. She's still my mama; I love her and thank God we have this time together.

My parents failed me in many ways; they are still my parents. I thank God for teaching me how to forgive them and keep His commandment to honor them. When I mess up as a mother, I pray my kids learn from my lead, and we all learn from mistakes of the past. Matthew 19:26 reminds me of a truth that sustains me. "Jesus looked at them and said, 'With men this is impossible, but with God all things are possible.'" (NKJV)

Jesus paid a tremendous price for us so we could have abundant life. He willingly took all of our sin on Himself and gave His life on the cross so we could be forgiven and have new life in Him.

Joyce Meyer

CHAPTER 16
WALKING FORWARD

Today, I thank God for life and everything I had to go through to get where I am now. If you never go through anything difficult, you never learn important lessons.

Today, I love working. I'm not worried about whether God loves me. Everything I went through in life is evidence that He loves and cares for me. I learned not to live off others' faith. I stopped letting people tell me what God won't do after everything I went through in my life from a child to now. God can do anything. All you have to do is believe.

Today, I'm not trying to get attention from man or please man. Today, I'm delivered from people. I feel good about myself. God delivered me from low self-esteem. According to Romans 8:37, we are more than conquerors through him that loved us.

After being bullied, lied on, used and abused I got to a point I started fighting back and speaking up for myself. I always had a kind heart, but I got to a point where I wanted people to think I was something that I wasn't. Even when I didn't take up for myself, some people thought they were using me for a long time. I wouldn't say nothing. I would shy away.

Then it became a habit of not knowing how to control my temper. Until one day, I told a guy I was on my way to fight him. I thought to myself, I'm gonna catch him unexpectedly. I went to sleep. I had a dream. I thought I was visiting someone in prison. After the visitation was over, I tried to leave and couldn't get out. A guard told me I was the inmate and in prison for attempted murder. After having a dream like that, I've been afraid to fight. Now when someone tries to cross me wrong, I follow Jesus. He said, "Father, forgive them for they knoweth not what they do." (Luke 23:34, KJV) Today, fighting is not an option for me. I learned how to pray for my enemies. I remember the battle is not mine—it's the Lord's.

Thank you Lord for delivering me from fighting.

Learning how to love me emerged slowly. I was always taught how to love and please other people, places and negative things. But today, I pray, "God let me see myself as you see me."

How beautifully He answers our prayers when we seek Him with a sincere and open heart.

He showed me I'm not a settle sister. I'm a mighty, wonderful, powerful woman of God. I'm more than a suicide attempt. I'm more than a rape victim. I'm more than depression. I'm more than sex before marriage. I'm more than a thief, liar.

It took me a long time to realize who I was. But today, I thank God because I'm not ashamed to tell anyone what I've been through. In my life today, I forgive all those who hurt me, raped me, lied, took advantage of me and let me down.

I am the CEO/Founder of Hurt Broken—Now Healed and Delivered Ministries. I'm an evangelist, reaching out to hurt and broke people. Telling my life story on how God healed and delivered me.

Today I'm my mother's caregiver in spite of all the heartache. She's still my mother. I cling to

Exodus 20:12, even when people tell me I'm crazy for taking care of her after she treated me bad for most of my life.

Today I'm a certified nurses' assistant. It teaches me to have a compassionate heart for people without destroying myself to please them.

I am a new creation because Jesus took my broken heart and made it a thing of the past. I am healed and delivered, moving forward in the destiny God prepared specifically for me from the beginning of time.

Jesus came to heal the brokenhearted. He did it in my life, and I am convinced he can do the same for any person. Your circumstances may look different—my story isn't yours. Details don't matter. His touch in your life does.

I'm no longer heartbroken. Can you say the same?

Bibliography

Margulies, S. (Producer), Haley, A. (Writer), & Chomsky, M. J. (Director). (1977). *Roots* [Motion Picture]. USA: ABC. Retrieved November 2015, from https://en.wikipedia.org/wiki/Roots_(miniseries)

Books are available at discounted prices for bulk purchases, sales promotions, fund-raising events or for educational purchases.

For more information about the author, to obtain special pricing or to schedule Teresa as a speaker for your event, please contact Teresa Tarpley at the address or phone number below.

Teresa Tarpley
Founder/CEO Hurt, Broken, Now Healed and Delivered Ministries
PO Box 50162
Fort Worth, TX 76105
(817) 210-7517
Email: minister.ttarpley@yahoo.com

ABOUT THE CO-AUTHOR

Lisa Bell lives in Granbury, Texas where she works as an editor for NOW Magazines, LLC. She also serves as a coach for Story Help Groups (formerly North Texas Christian Writers.) Lisa leads two writing groups, coaches individuals, edits and ghostwrites on a freelance basis. As the founder of Radical Women, she also helps writers with indie publishing.

Lisa has published more than 100 articles and several books, include her first novel, *Out of the Dungeon*. She is currently working on more books. You can learn more about Lisa, see her works in progress, or contact her by visiting www.bylisabell.com.

Made in the USA
San Bernardino, CA
16 August 2016